The Mighty Brontosaurus

Brianna Kaiser

BUMBA BOOKS™

LERNER PUBLICATIONS ◆ MINNEAPOLIS

Note to Educators

Throughout this book, you'll find critical-thinking questions. These can be used to engage young readers in thinking critically about the topic and in using the text and photos to do so.

Lerner Publications Company
An imprint of Lerner Publishing Group, Inc.
241 First Avenue North
Minneapolis, MN 55401 USA

For reading levels and more information, look up this title at www.lernerbooks.com.

Main body text set in Helvetica Textbook Com Roman.
Typeface provided by Linotype AG.

Library of Congress Cataloging-in-Publication Data

Names: Kaiser, Brianna, 1996– author.
Title: The mighty brontosaurus / Brianna Kaiser.
Description: Minneapolis : Lerner Publications, [2022] | Series: Bumba books - mighty dinosaurs | Includes bibliographical references and index. | Audience: Ages 4–7 | Audience: Grades K–1 | Summary: "What did brontosaurus look like? What body parts did it have? Readers become brontosaurus pros with the help of this fun book!"— Provided by publisher.
Identifiers: LCCN 2021010908 (print) | LCCN 2021010909 (ebook) | ISBN 9781728441078 (library binding) | ISBN 9781728444468 (ebook)
Subjects: LCSH: Apatosaurus—Juvenile literature.
Classification: LCC QE862.S3 K337 2022 (print) | LCC QE862.S3 (ebook) | DDC 567.913/8—dc23

LC record available at https://lccn.loc.gov/2021010908
LC ebook record available at https://lccn.loc.gov/2021010909

Manufactured in the United States of America
1-49879-49722-6/14/2021

Table of
Contents

Dino Giant!

Brontosaurus was a sauropod.

It is extinct.

It had a long neck and tail but short legs.

What other animals have long necks?

Each one was about the
length of two school buses.

8

It was heavy. Each one
weighed much more than
an elephant!

It ate only plants.

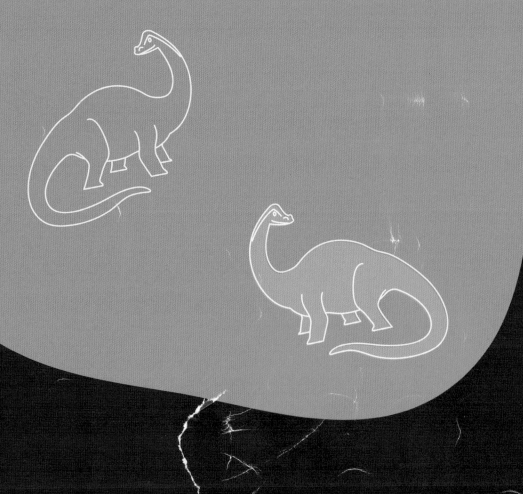

It may have used its long

neck to reach food.

How did a
long neck help
brontosaurus?

16

Scientists have found

many brontosaurus fossils

in North America.

Scientists once thought brontosaurus and apatosaurus were the same dinosaur. But fossils show differences between them.

apatosaurus

Scientists keep studying

fossils to learn more.

Parts of a Brontosaurus

neck

tail

legs

Picture Glossary

apatosaurus

a type of sauropod

extinct

no longer alive

fossil

a trace of a living animal from a long time ago

sauropod

a group of dinosaurs with long necks and tails

23

Learn More

Kaiser, Brianna. *The Mighty T. Rex.* Minneapolis: Lerner Publications, 2022.

Kelly, Erin Suzanne. *Dinosaurs.* New York: Children's Press, 2021.

Sabelko, Rebecca. *Apatosaurus.* Minneapolis: Bellwether Media, 2021.

Index

Photo Acknowledgments

Image credits: CSA Images/Getty Images, pp. 5, 23 (bottom right); neftali/Shutterstock.com, pp. 6, 23 (top right); Sergey Krasovskiy/Stocktrek Images/Getty Images, pp. 8–9; Michael Potter11/Shutterstock.com, p. 10; Michael Rosskothen/Shutterstock.com, p. 13; Science Photo Library/Alamy Stock Photo, pp. 14–15; Zack Frank/Shutterstock.com, p. 16; Daniel Eskridge/Shutterstock.com, pp. 19, 23 (top left); Kriengsak Wiriyakrieng/Shutterstock.com, pp. 20, 23 (bottom left); David Roland/Shutterstock.com, p. 22.

Cover: Karl Aage Isaksen/Shutterstock.com.